Disney · PIXAR

THE GOOD DINOSAUR

MUSIC BY MYCHAEL DANNA AND JEFF DANNA

ISBN 978-1-4950-5397-9

**Wonderland Music Company, Inc./
Pixar Music**

DISTRIBUTED BY

**HAL•LEONARD®
CORPORATION**
7777 W. BLUEMOUND RD. P.O. BOX 13819 MILWAUKEE, WI 53213

In Australia Contact:
Hal Leonard Australia Pty. Ltd.
4 Lentara Court
Cheltenham, Victoria, 3192 Australia
Email: ausadmin@halleonard.com.au

Visit Hal Leonard Online at
www.halleonard.com

HOMESTEAD

Music and Lyrics by MYCHAEL DANNA
and JEFF DANNA

Moderately

mp

Pedal ad lib. throughout

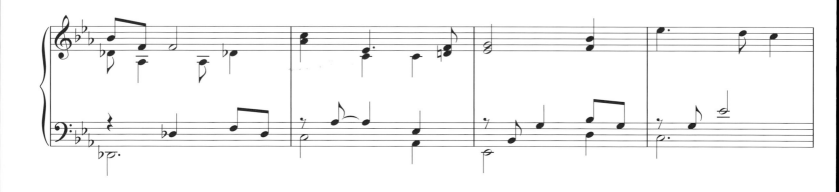

12

MAKE YOUR MARK

Music and Lyrics by MYCHAEL DANNA
and JEFF DANNA

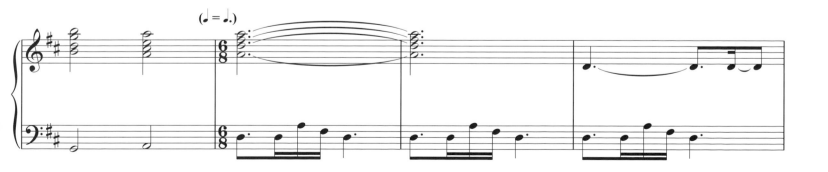

HELLO ARLO

Music and Lyrics by MYCHAEL DANNA
and JEFF DANNA

18

FAMILY STRUGGLE

Music and Lyrics by MYCHAEL DANNA
and JEFF DANNA

RESCUE

Music and Lyrics by MYCHAEL DANNA
and JEFF DANNA

UNEXPECTED FRIEND

Music and Lyrics by MYCHAEL DANNA
and JEFF DANNA

ORPHANS

Music and Lyrics by MYCHAEL DANNA
and JEFF DANNA

Moderately slow, expressively

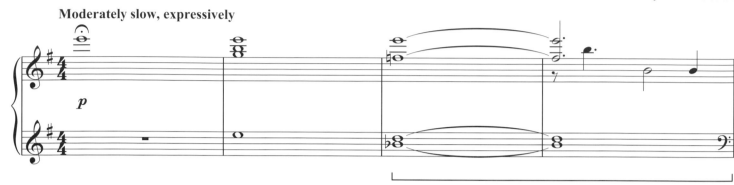

Pedal ad lib. throughout

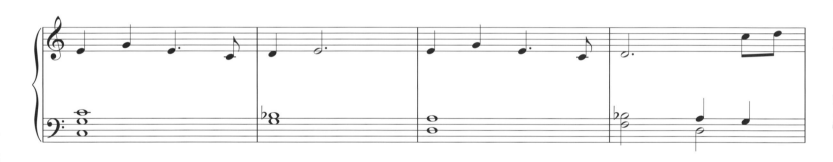

More slowly, freely

Tempo I

RUN WITH THE HERD

Music and Lyrics by MYCHAEL DANNA
and JEFF DANNA

34

Moderately slow ($\,\downarrow$. = $\,\downarrow$)

GOODBYE SPOT

Music and Lyrics by MYCHAEL DANNA
and JEFF DANNA

Slowly, expressively

p

Pedal ad lib. throughout

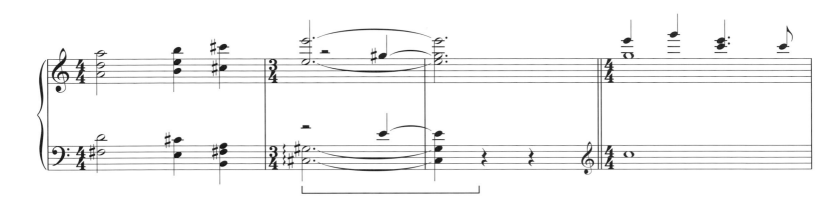

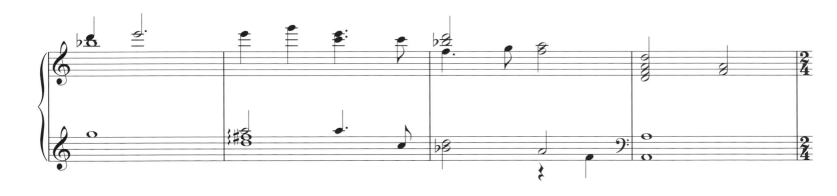

ARLO MAKES HIS MARK

Music and Lyrics by MYCHAEL DANNA
and JEFF DANNA

Moderately slow

mp

Pedal ad lib. throughout

rit.

HOMECOMING

Music and Lyrics by MYCHAEL DANNA
and JEFF DANNA

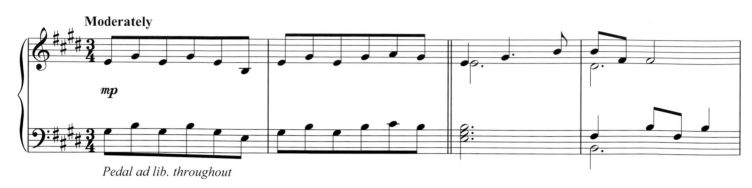